To Jonathan,

Always remember that God is crazy

in love with you!

Ken Metzger

The Potter's Perfect Piece

Kenneth Metzger
Illustrated by Denise Armstrong

WINEPRESS **WP** PUBLISHING

WinePress Publishing (PO Box 428, Enumclaw, WA 98022) functions only as book publisher. As such, the ultimate design, content, editorial accuracy, and views expressed or implied in this work are those of the author.

ISBN 13: 978-1-57921-876-8
ISBN 10: 1-57921-876-8
Library of Congress Catalog Card Number: 2006930666

Printed in Korea.

Dedication

To my beautiful wife, BG,
Without your strength, encouragement, and support,
I could never have traveled
the turbulent, terrifying road of despair named cancer.

And to my Lord Jesus Christ,
Without your example of facing fear head-on
with courage and focus on the goal,
I could not have "kept on keeping on."

And to all those who have persevered through the valleys,
gloried on the mountain peaks, and
held fast in the midst of chaos.
To you all, I say, "Well done.
Your courage is truly inspiring."

In a quiet town far, far away, there once lived a talented old man.
He was known far and wide for the beautiful things
he created from ordinary pieces of clay.
He was so talented in fact, that all who knew of his work just called him the Master.

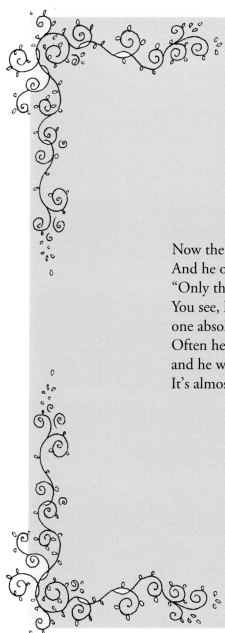

Now the old man knew a little secret that so many others did not know.
And he often whispered the secret to himself as he wandered around his dusty old shop.
"Only the very best clay will do to create a masterpiece, only the very best."
You see, he knew that in order to create a very special, one-of-a kind masterpiece,
one absolutely must use the very best clay available.
Often he would be right in the middle of making a beautiful piece,
and he would stop and say, "This clay seems to be fighting me.
It's almost as if it is alive and won't cooperate at all."

And so it was on this very warm, sunny day.
The old man carefully searched the shelves of his old, dusty shop,
looking for just the right piece of clay.
You see, it would soon be the good King's birthday.
The old man wanted to surprise Him with a very special gift.
It would show the King how much he loved Him,
and how much he appreciated all the King did for him.

"Ah, there you are," said the old man as he gently picked up
a small piece of clay from the shelf in the corner of his shop.
He examined it closely, working it through his talented fingers.
"You seem to be the right size and shape," the potter said.
"I believe you will become a very special piece for the King."

The old man continued to work the clay until it had softened up.
And as he worked the clay, his thoughts wandered to long ago when he first met the good King.
The King had a kind heart and always took care of his subjects.
He made sure they had warm homes to live in and plenty of food to eat.
He kept them safe from all harm.
The old man smiled, thinking of how much the King would enjoy this beautiful gift.

As the old man sat down to begin, he gently placed the piece of clay on his potter's wheel.

The excitement was growing in his heart.

The warm afternoon sun had brightened up the dusty old shop.

And then suddenly, without any warning, the piece of clay . . .

. . . came to life!

"Hey," he shouted. "Where am I? How did I get way over here?

I was minding my own business on the shelf for years, and suddenly when I woke up, I found myself over here. I demand to be put back right now.

Hey, old man, can't you hear me?"

And sure enough, the old man could not hear a word the clay was saying.

As he spoke to the old man, who as you remember could not hear him,
the clay felt a very nice sensation. The old man was gently rubbing him.
"Hey," said the clay, "that feels great, old man.
That spot has bothered me for years. Yeah, right there.
Now we're talking. Hey, old man, maybe you're not so bad after all.
I guess it will be all right if we hang out together for a while."

It seemed too good to be true. Sure enough, the massage was over way too soon.
The clay was beginning to worry now, as things suddenly seemed to be spinning
around him.
The world was getting blurry and out of focus.
"Please," he begged. "Please, old man, let me off this crazy ride.
I don't like this one bit. I am feeling sick to my stomach."
But again the old man could not hear him as he pedaled the wheel faster and faster.

Spinning wildly. Whirling out of control. Faster and faster.

"Mercy," he cried. "Mercy, please. How much more of this spinning can I take?

What have I done to you, old man?

Why Me ? Why now?"

But once again, the old man could not hear the piece of clay,

and he just kept on working.

As the clay continued to complain, he felt a sharp pain in his mid-section.
The old man's hands were shaping him. The pressure was starting to hurt him.
The old man was actually sticking his fingers and thumb into him.
"Ouch!" cried the clay. "Hey, cut that out. It hurts a lot!
Wow, you sure can be mean, old man."
But just as before, the old man could not hear a word the clay said.
He continued to work away.

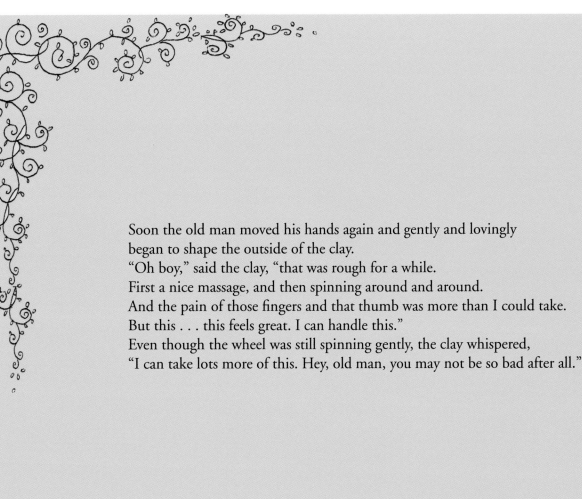

Soon the old man moved his hands again and gently and lovingly
began to shape the outside of the clay.
"Oh boy," said the clay, "that was rough for a while.
First a nice massage, and then spinning around and around.
And the pain of those fingers and that thumb was more than I could take.
But this . . . this feels great. I can handle this."
Even though the wheel was still spinning gently, the clay whispered,
"I can take lots more of this. Hey, old man, you may not be so bad after all."

Soon all of the spinning and shaping were over. The clay was too tired to complain any more. As he let out a weary sigh, he noticed a very beautiful orange glow off in the distance.

"How beautiful," he thought. "Like the sunset on a clear summer night."

And to his delight, the glow appeared to be drawing nearer and nearer.

Suddenly, he was right next to the glow and felt a very intense heat that brought him back to reality.

"Hey, old man," he shouted, "you aren't putting me in there. I'll die! It's hot in here! What have I done to deserve this, old man?"

As the door shut, the clay had fallen silent. It appeared that the end was here. He had given up. All was lost.

Over two hours had passed and as the clay finally awakened he found himself on the windowsill.

"I can't believe I survived that," he moaned.

"How much more can one piece of clay endure? Oh well, it sure is nice that it's finally over."

As he spoke, he overheard the old man talking to himself.

"I put you by the windowsill, my friend, because the perfect light of the sun will show if there are any flaws in you."

And as the old man closely examined the piece of clay he joyfully exclaimed, "There are none that I can see!"

The old man was really concentrating now.
His once shaky hands had grown steady.
His often failing eyes were fixed and determined.
Nothing else existed at this moment, and he would not be distracted.
The clay, having a soft smile on his face said,
"That kind of tickles. Old man, I am having trouble figuring you out.
Do you love me or hate me, old man?"
And as the last few brush strokes were being applied,
the old man seemed to almost whisper as he spoke . . .

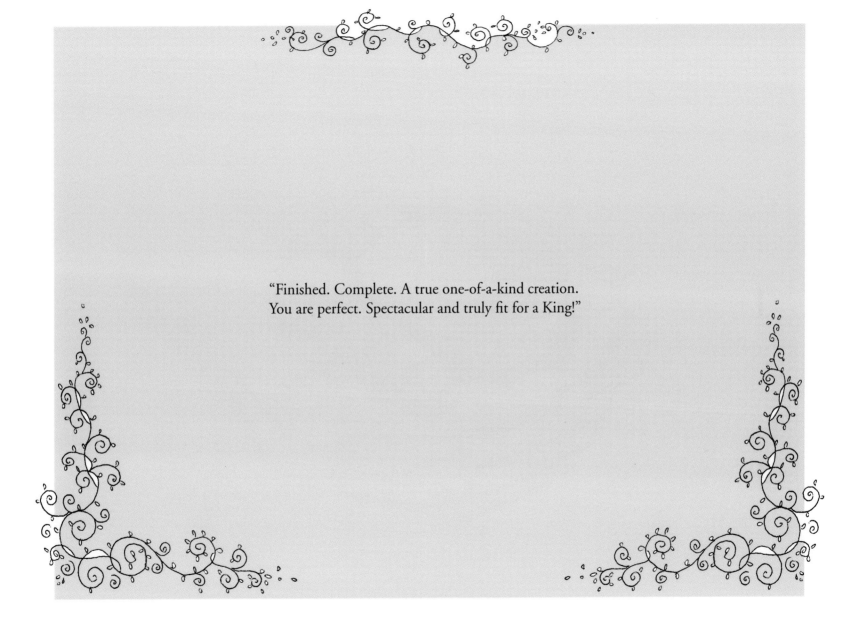

"Finished. Complete. A true one-of-a-kind creation.
You are perfect. Spectacular and truly fit for a King!"

The next day was the King's birthday.
The old man humbly approached the King carrying his masterpiece gently in his hands.
He had worked long and hard on this gift.
He had given his very best to the King.
And as he handed the King his present, the King exclaimed . . .

"How magnificent you are! And from an ordinary piece of clay."
As the King passed the mirror, the clay saw a beautiful tea cup.
"Wow!" he shouted. "You sure are a fine-looking tea cup.
Hey, wait a minute. That's me! I can't believe it.
I guess all of that trouble was worth it after all.
Look how much I've changed."

As the King held the cup in his hands, he whispered lovingly,
"I am truly sorry you had to suffer so much, my friend.
You see, it was the only way to change you.
Oh my beautiful one-of-a-kind,
I know the old man has put you through a lot.
I know there were good times and bad times.
I watched the massaging and spinning.
I saw the shaping, and oh my, that fire.
But it had to be allowed, my friend.
You were never intended to be just an ordinary piece of clay."

Discussion Page

In our story, the clay represents each of us and our lives. We are each unique—special, loved, and perfect for God's plan for our lives. Some pieces of clay will be perfect for a cup, some a saucer, and others a vase or water pitcher. We are all designed to be what God plans for us to be.

The old man represents life. God allows the old man of life to shape us, mold us, and form us. Sometimes life is kind, as in the kneading and massaging that feels so very good.

Sometimes life is out of control, as in the spinning.

Sometimes life is hard, as in the shaping.

And yes, sometimes we must even go through the fire. It is the only way we can become the finished cup of God's desire.

The King represents God. He loves us and allows the good times and the bad times in life to change us.

Final thoughts...

Jesus said "In this world, you will have trouble. But take heart.
I have overcome the world." (John 16:33)

The Bible says we all have sinned. We all have fallen short of God's plan.
The price for that sin is to be separated from God.
Forever. But God sent Jesus, His only Son, to pay the price for our sin on the
cross.
He died, was buried, and rose again to life on the third day.
He made it possible to spend forever with Him in Heaven.
If you will say you are sorry for your sin,
Ask Him to forgive you, and let Jesus be in charge of your life,
then you will be forgiven and one day be with Him forever.

To order additional copies of this title call:
1-877-421-READ (7323)
or please visit our web site at
www.winepressbooks.com

If you enjoyed this quality custom published book,

drop by our web site for more books and information.

www.winepressgroup.com

"Your partner in custom publishing."